Love That Journey For Me

Published by 404 Ink Limited
www.404Ink.com
@404Ink

Editing: Heather McDaid
Typesetting: Laura Jones
Cover design: Luke Bird
Co-founders and publishers of 404 Ink: Heather McDaid & Laura Jones

Print ISBN: 978-1-912489-34-3
Ebook ISBN: 978-1-912489-35-0

Printed and bound in Great Britain by Clays Ltd, Elcograf S.p.A.

404 Ink acknowledges support for this title from
Creative Scotland via the Crowdmatch initiative.

LOTTERY FUNDED

Love That Journey For Me

The Queer Revolution of *Schitt's Creek*

Emily Garside

Inklings

Contents

'I don't have a lot to my name right now, but I do have one thing'... a good warning that this book contains *Schitt's Creek* spoilers.

Spoiler alert!

If you have not watched *Schitt's Creek*, read no further! Come back once you've enjoyed the show.

Other spoilers:

As *Love This Journey For Me* discusses TV culture, numerous shows are discussed and some plot points are mentioned. If you would like to avoid spoilers for specific shows, please take note of these pages:

Introduction:
I feel like that needs
to be celebrated

The year is 2020 and everyone on social media is communicating via David Rose GIFs. That's how it felt, anyway. Lines from hit TV show *Schitt's Creek* became catchphrases, 'Ew, David' was a fitting response to 2020's endless lockdowns, sweaters in summer felt a sensible option, and many wondered if Moira Rose's premiere dress was 'too much' for our first night out after the pandemic. Amidst it all, the audience was rooting for a gay love story as the central endgame love affair. It felt big, ground-breaking, on this scale. And it was all from a seemingly innocuous Canadian TV show that had mostly flown under the radar.

Schitt's Creek had felt like TV's best kept secret.

1

Then, with the world on pause due to the COVID-19 pandemic, it became the show everyone was talking about, the happy tonic to the reality of the world. For me, it was a show that reached out at time I needed it. Notoriously late to every party, I pride myself on not being last to this one; I spent much of 2019 telling friends and colleagues to watch it. Having lost my job, it became one of those little slices of joy to escape into. As a scholar of queer culture, I started to lose myself in the queer narratives it told (also as a distraction from my academic work on… queer narratives). More importantly, I found lots of myself, and kinship, and hope I needed, in that show. I can pinpoint the exact moment I fell in love with it (the season two finale), the moment I knew that as a queer, academic and musicals nerd I needed to write about it (when Patrick gets the part of the Emcee in the town's amateur production of *Cabaret*); but also the moments I felt most seen (David's coming out) and most changed (Patrick's coming out). And in what was a lonely year in many ways, it felt like I was adding some more members to my chosen family.

The idea behind the show is a charming fish-out-of-water story on the surface. The wealthy Rose family – parents Johnny and Moira Rose, and adult kids David and Alexis – lose their money and everything they own due to a crooked accountant. Except one asset, that is – not the children, as soap actress Moira asks – a town that

Johnny, former video store chain owner, bought as a joke birthday present years prior.

Moving to Schitt's Creek, they relocate to the town's dilapidated motel and spend their first year trying to escape, and the next few building lives there instead. They don't immediately fit in, though the town's generous inhabitants help them rebuild their lives; though not their former lives, much better, new lives instead. Between running for town council (Moira), helping run the motel they live in (Johnny), going back to school (Alexis), and taking over the general store (David), they slowly become part of the town, and better people in the process.

The show managed to occupy a space of both slow burn hit and overnight success all at once. The brainchild of father-son duo Eugene and Dan Levy, it found its home on the Canadian Broadcasting Corporation (CBC), first airing in January 2015. Not a network known for comedy output, it was what Eugene Levy remembered to be an opportune moment – they were looking for a network, the network were looking for a rebrand. Finding a home on CBC seemed an almost fatalistic stroke of luck that ultimately allowed the show freedom and understanding to tell the stories they wanted to.

The freedom extended to other areas: *Schitt's Creek* wasn't an out-of-the-box immediate hit. It did steady numbers of around 1 million viewers on first airing. This held across season two, which the network greenlit before the first season had even aired in another bold and supportive move. It wasn't until the fourth season that the show broke 2 million viewers an episode. On another network the same grace period probably wouldn't have been offered; nor perhaps the boldness of support for the their ideas – from the title that some US broadcasters struggled to say on air due to its sneakily profane inflection, to the inclusive and ground-breaking LGBTQ+ content that would also characterise it.

For many new viewers, the show and its creators had come seemingly from nowhere. Dan Levy had not followed directly in his father's footsteps; while he had a number of small acting credits, he had moved into presenting early in his career – known for his time as an MTV Canada presenter. Eugene Levy has worked consistently but often in the background for several decades. Despite being well known to many – in particular the loyal fans of Christopher Guest's films, or for a generation being a face of SCTV, and to a younger generation as the infamous Jim's Dad from *American Pie* – Eugene Levy was, as with most great character actors, probably known to most as 'that guy from that thing' with a quick look to IMDB to remind them exactly what.

Despite the impressive résumés of those involved with the show, they were largely unknown to the wider TV-watching world, especially the younger actors. Catherine O'Hara, who plays Moira, shares Eugene

Levy's impressive back catalogue, being another long-standing member of Christopher Guest's films. O'Hara's chameleon-like acting skills were discovered by a new generation when the internet learned that Moira Rose was also Kevin's mum from *Home Alone*. This, teamed with a number of the cast being relatively unknown, removed preconceptions; viewers couldn't assume what to expect from the Rose family and the town's residents.

It played in the show's favour, achieving steady ratings, and a handful of awards (MTV and GLAAD), gaining some, but not massive, recognition. The move to Netflix brought the show to new dizzying heights.

By the end of 2020, *Schitt's Creek* swept the board at the Emmys. It took five seasons to get a nomination, and here this seemingly innocuous show won 11, including for all the leading cast members, and Outstanding Series. All for a show that ended by placing a gay wedding – and a gay romantic happy ending, at that – at its core. But how did they manifest this? And why does it matter?

At its heart, *Schitt's Creek* is a story of love and acceptance. This is what makes it a hit. Whether it's considering what is involved in accepting who you are, who your family is, where you end up in life, or all of the above. Themes of unconditional love, healing, and family all carry the show forward, challenging conventional views of what that looks like – the idea of family in the show is actually very dependent on the idea of a *chosen* family, something vital to many queer relationships. Befitting of its title, the town itself is also central to the show's message, the huge cast of hilarious and kind patrons are there to also connect with fans, casual viewers, while often ending up making some political statements in the process that you might not expect.

Schitt's Creek saved me, and it also brought me joy at a time when I needed it. By the time I watched the finale (very late to the party this time) at one of the lowest moments of my life personally, I'd become almost evangelical in my belief that you find this show when you need it. So, just like the show gave us new queer stories and things that we needed, I wanted to tell the story of what that meant, and why that matters.

Chapter 1:
A town without prejudice

Schitt's Creek is the world Dan Levy wants to live in. That's how Catherine O'Hara described it in an interview with *The Guardian*, adding, 'And I do too.' The idea is simple: what if these characters were able to exist somewhere free from the wider prejudices of the world? That Schitt's Creek (the town) is a place where prejudice practically doesn't exist is a brilliant instance of how *Schitt's Creek* (the show) managed to lead by example and ask, simply: what if the world looked like this instead?

Stories about homophobia, along with other forms of prejudice, have been needed to right the wrongs of previous TV and film narratives, whether deliberately homophobic, or because it was culturally acceptable, covertly or overtly. Storylines challenging that have been a vital part of queer visibility, but perhaps the next evolution on that journey is to start imagining what stories might be told if we simply take homophobia out of the equation.

Considering some examples, we can look back to the '90s, when shows like *Friends* held running jokes that Chandler must be gay due to his mannerisms and his upbringing, or we see insinuations that Ross has 'turned' his wife gay. We also see Ross being upset that his son enjoys playing with a Barbie over a generic, more 'manly' doll, or we see him confused and conflicted when Rachel, the mother of his child, wants to hire a male nanny.

The Simpsons made a lazy homophobic joke in Homer taking Bart to steel mill The Anvil to show him what 'real men' look like, then finding it populated by Village-People lookalikes. Or 'progressive' shows like *Sex and the City* making light around the tired jibe that bisexuals don't really exist. Later, *How I Met Your Mother* ends up constantly fetishizes lesbian relationships for Barney's entertainment, or uses it as a running joke about friends Lily and Robin. Even '90s classic *American Pie,* starring our own Eugene Levy, has its homophobic moments that were deemed acceptable and funny at the time.

Shows that carry more representation aren't completely free of fault either, such as *Glee* which fell back on clichés and problematic tropes like invalidating bisexuality. Even *Will and Grace,* which made huge strides for representation, constantly made jokes at the expense of lesbian characters.

And don't forget *Gilmore Girls* which did not actually allow camp receptionist Michel to be an gay character until its revived episodes in 2016. In their defence, the writers did try to make character Sookie a lesbian before being denied by the network, indicating a blatant systemic homophobia in TV production. There are many more I could list.

Removing homophobic elements such as these from fictional narratives could free writers to tell other stories. If we imagine *Schitt's Creek* falling foul to more tired, arguably homophobic tropes of the previous decades, we might have seen David moving to town and experiencing multiple encounters of homopobia; Patrick, who David is yet to meet and fall in love with, would realise his attraction to David despite living as a straight man, and his coming out could have been diverted, or dominated by him dealing with external judgement. Even Jake, who enjoys sexual encounters with both David and Stevie around the same time, may have spent more time fending off ignorant comments than deciding who his next 'throuple' might be. Thankfully, *Schitt's Creek* is the antithesis of these narrative pitfalls.

Instead, we see queer love stories and hookups unfold without fear or consequences of prejudice; queer people are just seen as that: people. To watch David and Patrick clumsily develop a relationship and stumble through variously typical roadblocks on their way to marriage, the usual ups and downs of any relationship, shouldn't feel quite such a television storyline revelation – yet it does.

For queer viewers, it's a chance to see their stories told as normal stories, which – we already know – they are, but these queer romantic narratives are so often filtered through the eyes of writers *and* characters with prejudice, those simply blind to a non-heteronormative relationship. More importantly, queer viewers get to see a happy, relatively carefree version of a gay love story, something rarely seen in cultural portrayals. From '90s AIDS stories like *Philadelphia* that implied that gay stories sat as only warnings to tragic stories like *Brokeback Mountain,* or tragic endings for characters in TV like Willow and Tara in *Buffy the Vampire Slayer.* Even queer-led shows like *The L Word* and *Queer as Folk* find themselves filled with tragic endings and early deaths for characters more frequently than in 'straight TV'. Whatever you do, don't be a queer character in a soap opera show – queer characters everywhere from *Emmerdale* to *Days of Our Lives* have met untimely, unhappy, and unnecessary ends.

This isn't to say that prejudice doesn't exist in the *Schitt's Creek* universe. A variety of vague references keep audiences aware that the show is a reflection of the real world, not a separate utopia. David's stance on team sports, when he is forced to take part in the town's amateur (and hilarious) baseball game – we are divided enough politically, for example, without further segregation through sport teams – feels like a succinct one-line summary of what could have been a heavy-handed political polemic. For the six years the show was on the air, it was a needed antidote to the often frightening political and societal shifts in our own world, beyond the town's limits.

A clear indicator that *Schitt's Creek* is an oasis within the wider world is seen as soon as episode two of the first season. When motel employee Stevie mentions a truck party to David and his sister Alexis, he replies, 'No thanks, I'm not in the mood to be the victim of a hate crime tonight.' David, whose sexuality is, at this point, unknown to the audience, automatically becomes defensive and scolds Stevie for this invitation, on the basis of his appearance, mannerisms, and his likely past unpleasant experiences because of them. What actually happens when he turns up is an awkward conversation with Twyla and David after they are offered a beer bong and they demonstrate a distinct lack of prowess in drinking it. Nobody else seems to notice his presence or care about his appearance. Rather than the homophobic slurs, or potential attacks he fears (which have likely happened to him numerous times before in David's past) the townsfolk are more concerned with drinking than the newcomers at their party. It becomes clear that this middle-of-nowhere-town doesn't have any prejudice, which makes a powerful point, both about how the world could be and the impact it has on people. By showing a hate-free, fun-filled truck party full of accepting, small town revellers instead of queer suffering for the sake of narrative progression, Levy is leading by example.

Levy knows that the queer viewer will recognise the very real, lived fear that David has, reflecting the experience of common prejudice many queer people are forced to tolerate. Even the visuals of the town stir up these connotations. Many a queer viewer will see the quirky town bar, the Wobbly Elm, and immediately feel a familiar tension, the kind that comes with going inside a very particular kind of straight venue. Any kind of Very Straight venue can have that effect, especially on someone who knows themselves to be 'visibly queer'.

The Wobbly Elm is a subversion of TV's village pub as a location. It looks like the type of place queer people could be fearful of entering; in fact, it hosts a gay bachelor party, and is where Ronnie – a middle-aged Black butch lesbian – picks up a date with a woman, while garage owner Bob doesn't manage to; a great twist on the instinctual feeling that pubs such as these could hold hostility. It's a simple and brilliantly strange utopia.

Although the main focus on prejudice, and its apparent absence from Schitt's Creek, circles homophobia, it's a town removed from, but not unaware of, wider prejudice too.

This is seen mainly in the Roses' Jewish identity which is simply integrated into the fabric of the show – David and Alexis comment on their Bat/Bar Mitzvahs and Johnny talks unselfconsciously about Hebrew School. We're made aware of this part of their identity, and much like the queer characters, it's a significant part of their identity, but not the sole defining characteristic, nor a plot point.

Early on, Bob fears accidentally being seen as racist and asks if he's allowed to say 'Jewish' (Johnny reassures him, yes, in that context, it's not racist). There is a hefty dose of the real world; that Bob of Bob's Garage, in a small town, might not be the most politically correct rings true, as does his genuine fear of offending. It also highlights that the people of the town aren't blind to difference – of heritage, sexuality, or race – prejudice isn't removed from this equation by pretence it doesn't exist, but in the town's refusal to respond negatively to normality.

They also play a realistic line in self-deprecating humour which makes the world of the show feel authentic. In a nice parallel several seasons apart, both Johnny and David use a need for kosher food (or in David's case, wine) as a means to get out of an awkward social situation. Johnny to distract from a poker game not going his way, David to get out of what appears to be an orgy. Is this the first time on television kosher wine has been used as an excuse to get out of an orgy? Possibly. There's also a lowkey running joke around Johnny's love of pork chops and a nudge to his less-than-kosher approach to religion. Or, David referring to himself as a 'deeply embittered and mildly Hebraic looking elf'.

This form of humour is also seen in David in reference to sexuality or gender expression. Likewise, Moira and Alexis frequently mock David's sexual misadventures, but in a fond, familial manner that siblings and parents might; it's never directly about his sexuality, just his unfortunate choices. It's the same for fashion – Stevie comments on his wearing a leather sweater in August, Patrick laughs along with his dad about David's fashion choices; in (lovingly) mocking David's clothing it's always in the vein of his clothing being outlandish, never a negative comment relating to gender or sexuality. In fact, that side of David's fashion sense is never commented on at all. Always walking a careful line between commentary that is realistic, but not crossing a line into, for example, negative commentary that could come from David's occasional enjoyment in wearing a skirt, as many other TV shows could be prone to do. This town doesn't engage with small-minded attitudes that exist elsewhere. *Schitt's Creek* allows normal to simply *be*, and to not have to defend itself as such.

The contrast between the small-minded and the small-town is most clearly seen in the season two finale, when Moira and Johnny run into old friends at dinner. These 'friends', who they haven't heard from since losing their fortune, spend most of the dinner mocking the hilariously-named town they drove through on the way, and complaining about the restaurant. Their taunts are snobbish and juvenile all at once – mocking the town name, pointing to the low-quality food and drink, and a thinly veiled disdain for Mayor Roland Schitt, and his wife Jocelyn. These former friends are a stark reminder of what the world outside the town is like: judgmental, cruel and ultimately selfish.

Johnny tells them just how welcoming, kind and generous their new friends have been, pointing out how they shared 'what little they have' with his family. It's at once a cruel reminder that in the 'real world', Johnny and his family have been abandoned by everyone they knew, as well as a reminder of what is possible with a shift to kindness. The key difference between their old friends and new ones is that the Schitts would never judge the Roses based on what they did or didn't have, and the Roses are as welcome in their town as anyone. The influence of the town already clear on Johnny when he declares triumphantly, 'It's Schitt's Creek.' Instead of dinner with their old 'friends', they return to town and dance joyously in a barn with their family, and their new, real friends.

It's a joy to see this town live exactly as they wish. We see this primarily through the story arcs of David and Patrick, whose queer love story has had such a profound impact on

Schitt's Creek viewership and potentially wider entertainment culture, but also on the other characters within the show. From the slightly eccentric town residents like Ray (the town's estate agent/travel agent/photographer/Christmas tree salesman and so much more), or Bob, living their quirky lives uninhibited, to the town being run by Roland Schitt, who clearly embraces a 'go your own way' attitude to both life and Mayoral duties. Everyone manages to follow their heart towards fulfilment, regardless of what the wider world might deem as 'success'.

In career directions, the town inspires Mutt's off-grid existence, Twyla choosing the café over more affluent opportunities, and Stevie choosing the motel over a life outside of the town. Even Ted, the town's highly-educated vet, is a strangely delightful man embraced for his animal puns, and eventually pursuing his dreams studying in the Galapagos. There's no sense of anyone being told they're wasting their potential, quite the opposite – by doing what makes them happy, they're all fulfilling it.

It's against this backdrop that the Roses thrive too. Alexis breaks free from her previous lifestyle of wild misadventures to return to high school, go to college and pursue a career path she loves. The safety of the town, free from judgment, allows her to do this. Sure, there is friendly sibling mockery at her first day at school, and during her lice outbreak, but there's also genuine support and pride from her brother on her long-earned graduation. Taking Alexis away from the people whose only currency was judgment, seen clearly when her old friends also roll through town in season three, allows her to actually be who she can be and wants to be instead. And while Alexis will eventually leave, it's the town itself that makes her the person able to do that, as the best person she could be.

Even Moira and Johnny find this. They are no longer 'Johnny and Moira Rose', judged by their home, awards, holidays, golf handicap. Here, they're the same as everyone else (no matter how much Moira still tries to stand out through her outrageous finery). As much as their kids, they both need the time to figure out who they were – something lost along the way. It's the town's influence that lets them reconnect to their truest selves. Moira goes back to acting with the self-assurance to reclaim what was taken from her, Johnny starts a new business that comes from a place of true altruism, and this allows him to help his new friends.

For David, much of his character arc centres on his ability to find a functional relationship – and ultimately the love of his life – after the damage of his past. The narrative around David's past relationships is that they generally were not good people, that he made repeated bad choices. When Moira talks to David about the impact Patrick has had on him, she talks of 'drawing a line' under his previous life of terrible relationships. It is the safety of the town that plays a big part in David's growth, who is self-described 'damaged goods', to help him heal and find true happiness. At the end of the show, David's decision on where his future lies too speaks to that positive influence; who wouldn't, given the chance, ultimately choose safety where they feel most themselves? There is an important connection between his choice of Schitt's Creek over their old home of New York, and that he tells Patrick in their wedding vows that he feels safe with him. Whether he knows it or not, the town, as much as Patrick, created that feeling – it wasn't possible to have one without the other.

For Patrick, it is moving to the town that, in every sense, allows him to be who he really is. Whether you read it as his relocation, his meeting David as a revelation about his sexuality, or his coming to terms with it, the town and its safety plays a huge part. It asks the question, if Patrick had lived somewhere like that his whole life, would he have spent so long in a doomed relationship with ex-fiancée Rachel? Would he have had to wait so long to, as he puts it, 'understand what right felt like'? Would he have found David had they met elsewhere? Patrick explains his reluctance to come out to his parents by how comfortable he'd gotten with David and his family in the town. The town has created this almost-perfect oasis where someone like Patrick can quietly learn about, accept and act on his true sexuality.

And, most importantly, a lesson from both Patrick and David's stories: when hate and fear are taken out of the equation, when you have a place of acceptance: love wins.

Chapter 2:
Queering the sitcom

Most people in their 30s and above remember the first 'gay [insert activity here]' on TV – for millennials, shows like the seminal *Queer as Folk* and *The L Word* offered one slice of 'Gay Life' on TV. This was also the time before streaming services and prolific broadband, so all of these ground-breaking shows were viewed on late night TV or smuggled in on VHS and DVDs, hidden away from flatmates or parents. On mainstream TV there were very few queer people, or, at least, visibly queer people.

Levy's personal influences are clearly infused – as we'll get to – in the storytelling of *Schitt's Creek*, and he takes it one step further in queering them. 'Queering' in the broader sense – more than just re-working the central love story into a gay one, but in re-evaluating and shifting to a new set of values – not governed by heter-onormative values or the 'rules' of the TV stories that accompany them.

Queer life experience is different; queer cultural experience is different. Why not reframe stories *using* existing tropes rather than cookie-cutter it instead? That's also what 'queering' means: to disrupt, reframe, challenge and question how it's always been done.

But how has it always been done?

Ellen Degeneres came out in the '90s and at the same time, her character Ellen Morgan, on the eponymous TV show, became the first gay leading character on a prime time sitcom in the USA. Her now infamous 'Yep, I'm Gay' *TIME* cover has become a visual landmark of this moment in queer representation, both on screen and off. *Will & Grace* brought in the 2000s, redressing the balance of blockbuster shows like *Friends* and *Seinfeld* – which, as much as '90s kids like me still fondly remember them, often used queer people as the punchline. None of those shows were actively trying to hurt queer people (I hope) – *Friends* did have recurring gay characters in Carol and Susan, *Seinfeld* won a GLAAD award for the episode 'The Outing' (1993), in which Jerry and George are assumed to be gay. Neither of these meet today's inclusive standards, but I think were trying, at their time. Times change, and so too does queer storytelling.

Will & Grace was a gay-led show that kicked down more than a few doors. In season two there is an episode about cutting a gay kiss from a TV show, causing characters Jack and Will to petition to the network to reinstate it (and stage their own live-on-air kiss). It's still an active conversation in many writers rooms: how much is too much in showing intimacy between men? Given that episode of *Will & Grace* aired in 2000, it's also a striking illustration of the importance of shows giving airtime to queer stories, and that these conversations persist.

While there remain notable issues, and the journey for strong representation has been a long one, *Schitt's Creek* joins an ever-growing repertoire of positive queer visibility on mainstream TV, from shows like *Brooklyn Nine-Nine*, the police sitcom which integrated queer representations into its characters – Captain Raymond Holt and his partner Kevin, Rosa Diaz coming out as bisexual – without ever explicitly framing itself as a 'queer' show, or *The Good Place* which embraced sexual fluidity and acceptance as just part of the make-up of its world – Eleanor Shellstrop alluding to bisexuality, albeit never being shown on screen. Or for shows like fairytale-twist *One Day at A Time* and family mockumentary *Modern Family*, where their queer characters are an integral part of the narrative and aren't glossed over or ignored in terms of identity, nor the importance of the issues they face.

In TV drama, the inclusion of queer characters has steadily become more mainstream, led by writers like Shonda Rhimes whose shows *Greys Anatomy, Station 19* and *How to Get Away with Murder* have all showcased diverse storylines across the series. Long-running ensemble TV series in North America have often been forerunners of inclusivity, including Canadian stalwart teen drama *Degrassi* which explored many queer storylines aimed at a younger audience, from Marco Del Rossi in *Degrassi the Next Generation* through to Paige Michalchuck, girlfriend Alex Nuñez, and trans and genderqueer characters Adam Torres and Yael Baron.

Russell T Davies' *Queer as Folk* burst onto Channel 4 at the start of the new millennium. The (mis)adventures of Stuart and Vince – along with occasional hookup Nathan – looked set to change how gay stories were told on TV. It was the first post-AIDS gay drama, and one that deliberately never mentioned the epidemic. It was hedonistic, irreverent, and very British in its sense of humour. *Queer as Folk* didn't hold back in showing the sexual side of gay life, as well as showing what the gay community looked like.

What the gay community looked like in TV, however, was often cast firmly within tragedy, if not the 'light-hearted' punchline. The 'bury your gays' trope refers to the fact that often gay characters will meet a tragic end, from Willow's girlfriend Tara on *Buffy the Vampire*

Slayer to Matt Fielding in *Melrose Place,* even Loras in *Game of Thrones* (which might get a pass, as death is fairly indiscriminate in Westeros). Britain's first lesbian kiss – Brookside's Margaret Clemence and Beth Jordache – saw one character's plot end in death. People may die in soaps all the time – as Moira could attest – but the proportion was alarmingly high. Dan Levy recalls being asked not to make 'anything terrible' happen to Patrick when he joined the show, which might seem like an over-protective reaction, but within its context, it's a logical fandom fear.

An important note in this trajectory of gay stories – on TV and beyond – is the kind of 'interrupted history', particularly for gay men's stories as a result of AIDS-era storytelling. Suddenly, for over a decade, all the storytelling around gay men got channelled into AIDS stories. This was vital in many ways: AIDS stories were a form of activism and memorial, key in raising awareness and the collective grief running through the community. Arguably, given there are examples of 'happy ending' stories in film and theatre particularly, it feels like stories were 'just getting going' and there was hope of that 'happy ending' narrative, when things were derailed. It's also not a huge leap to see the moral associations made by many such approaches.

For a while, in any gay narrative, it felt like every character had to have a conversation about HIV/AIDS at some point. HIV of course remains an important issue, however, it's refreshing that not every story centring gay characters has to incorporate that now, that we can have stories that are purely about love and sex. That in itself feels like forward movement in representation.

It's also an important re-steering of narratives for audiences and creatives. For queer people currently in their 30s, they probably had a constant awareness of AIDS when they were children, an everlasting presence like white noise. It became a marker of the 'bad things' that happened to queer people, which could contribute to the internalised fear and shame that comes with those narratives being the first, and often only, exposure of queer representation. Consciously or subconsciously, that has impacted a generation. And so out of those ashes, the need for a counter-narrative that isn't all-consumed by the fear of illness isn't surprising.

These TV legacies of queer representation don't exist in isolation, but in the wider web of queer culture. Before TV could, theatre told gay stories. Mart Crowley's play *The Boys in the Band* (1968) is considered the first 'mainstream' Broadway play to be about openly gay men. *Cabaret* – well known to *Schitt's Creek* – was a mixed set of progress and sideways steps in its depiction of queer characters. Later, *La Cage Aux Folles* (1984) became an early contender for positive depictions of gay relationships, and gay happy endings. There's a whole host of queer stories taking place in theatre that eventually fuelled the revolutions beyond the stage.

For the Dan Levys to be able to tell their stories, we first needed to see those who hid their queerness for the stage (Tennessee Williams) and for the page (Christopher Isherwood). There were those who stayed closeted to the wider public like E.M. Forster, and those who were outed and couldn't finish what they started, like Oscar Wilde. Without them, there may be no *Schitt's Creek*.

There's a speech in Larry Kramer's play *The Normal Heart* which begins 'I belong to a culture' that goes on to list gay men who have impacted culture: Walt Whitman, Herman Melville, Tennessee Williams, Byron, E.M. Forster, Lorca, Auden, and so on, itself a call-back to Oscar Wilde's speech at his indecency trial for homosexuality in 1895 which comments on 'great works of art like those of Shakespeare and Michelangelo.' Both are about the debt of those who went before, and a hidden culture made visible, thanks to their suffering. There is a through-line of queer culture that in its hidden histories and struggles becomes interconnected. In being a queer person consuming media, we are forever constructing our own histories. When your history isn't the dominant one, you have to pull together the bits and pieces until you can construct a story that feels like your own. It feels like *Schitt's Creek* was doing exactly that, acknowledging its place on that line. The show also provides another step on that long path, one that meets those who might continue to say 'I belong to a culture', and they can add new names. Names that make sure queer culture is no longer hidden or presented only as misery and suffering.

Schitt's Creek is able to exist, and further push the way TV tells queer stories, because of all that went before it – the good and the bad. In existing, and pushing those boundaries, it is a part of paving the way for what comes next.

Chapter 3:
Wine, not the label

Coming out stories: the sequel

When we talk about queer narratives in TV, coming out tends to be the focus – the key moment in a character's journey, often a central plot device. In *Schitt's Creek*, we see a sensitive and honest portrayal of Patrick's coming out, which both addresses his own experience, and that of his parents and those around him. But he is not alone. David, too, has to come out. This is important for two reasons: firstly, it identifies David as pansexual, a vital element of his character, and the kind of representation the show offers; secondly, it addresses an important element of life for queer people: that they never stop coming out.

Lazy and, sadly, rife storytelling often shows queer people coming out in a blaze of rainbows and/or trauma, and then it's resolved and done. The truth is, coming out is a lifelong task. Every new job, new friend, new date and – yes – new town, you have to come out over and over again. Even if people assume – like Stevie does with David – you have to eventually confirm or deny. Obviously, the first time is significant for everyone, but the never-ending coming out is important to address, as is how it's received.

For David, coming out to Stevie, and therefore the show's viewers, as pansexual, is particularly significant in TV narrative terms. His coming out also includes another, often overlooked, point – that his parents also 'come out' in talking about their queer son. While it shouldn't be directly compared, parents 'coming out' to friends – new and old – about their queer children also run a risk of judgment and rejection. Johnny and Moira, finding their feet in a strange new town, likely share the same worries as their son – would their new friends reject them, or even be hostile? David's revealed sexuality could have consequences for them all in another context, and that's an important broader point subtly made by *Schitt's Creek* – homophobia often affects more than just the person receiving the judgement. Until the town's true colours of acceptance show, Moira and Johnny share some of the coming out anxiety.

David's storyline illustrate's Johnny and Moira's accept-ance first and foremost, yes, but also the struggles that parents sometimes go through. The Roses are accepting, however, seeing Johnny confused and concerned feels an authentic reaction. Consistent characterisation shows that Moira, the 'showbiz mom' and the younger of the two, is more laid back, reminding Johnny that David's 'sexually adventurous' nature is 'not a phase'. It's cleverly structured across the episode in that Johnny is surprised by – on many levels – finding Stevie and David in bed together, but he's also relieved that maybe David is starting a relationship with her.

Johnny's first conversation with Moira makes it appear that perhaps he isn't entirely accepting of David's sexuality. This shifts later in the episode when Johnny talks to Roland at a party, telling him that his son is pansexual. After Roland gets his head around pansexual not being a cookware fetish, Johnny asks, 'Wouldn't it be easier to just pick a gender?' Johnny is obviously concerned for his son's potential unhappiness. He is imperfect in his approach.

Roland's response is probably the moment the show truly started to embody the important queer narrative it would become – 'We can't tell our kids who to love.' In so doing, he firmly drew a line in the sand for the show. It is in typical fashion as funny as it is endearing – Roland is both stoned and eating barbeque in a typically inelegant manner. For me, this was a defining moment in the show's message of importance. Perhaps because it comes from Roland, who is in every sense an unlikely source of wisdom. Perhaps for me, because I grew up surrounded by 'Rolands', working class, slightly rough around the edges men, it meant more to hear that kind of acceptance from him, rather than the 'from another world' and also slightly 'too good to be true' Johnny Rose. Perhaps it's also wishing there was a 'Roland' around to shrug, tell everyone else to accept it and go back to eating barbeque and getting stoned. It's also that as Mayor, Roland is unofficially speaking for the town and what it stands for. In the throwaway moments of easy inclusivity is where the hope lies.

The wine, not the label

David's pansexuality is explored in several ways across the show. Johnny refers to the 'college years', Moira reiterates 'it's not a phase'. David will casually refer to partners of all genders, and his boyfriend will talk about his 'colourful' dating history. But it's the now famous 'wine, not the label' speech that stands out.

While shopping for dinner party supplies, Stevie asks about David's sexual orientation in a non-judgmental way, using wine preferences as a metaphor; a valid enough question having just had sex with David, previously assuming he was gay. The conversation deserves a full quotation in all its glory:

David: I do drink red wine, but I also drink white wine. And I've also been known to sample the occasional rosé. And a couple summers back I tried a Merlot that used to be a Chardonnay, which got a bit complicated.

Stevie: So yeah, you're just really open to all wines.

David: I like the wine and not the label. Does that make sense?

Stevie immediately accepts his answer. The 'wine, not the label' speech has become iconic for many reasons, in all that it symbolises: an out, pansexual character who is unapologetic, and not judged for it. David's way of framing the description is brilliant in its directness, but also descriptiveness.

The neat summary, 'I like the wine not the label', has understandably been adopted by queer people of all 'labels' because it neatly fits any number of sexual and gender expressions. It's also a lovely update of something from an iconic queer text, Evelyn Waugh's *Brideshead Revisited*, a story centred on complex questions of sexuality, relationships and identity. A number of wine metaphors run throughout, with Anthony Blanche saying, 'I know your tastes', while ordering wine for Charles Ryder, whose sexuality is ambiguous across the novel.

Although David never refers to himself with a label, it's of note that his dad does. Despite the emphasis on 'the wine and not the label', it's significant that Johnny names David as pansexual because queer identities other than gay or lesbian are so rarely talked about on television. There's power in naming them to the audience, both in seeing a diversity of queer identities presented unproblematically and that David is consistently pansexual across the show, and not just as a poor taste gag or plot point.

Jake is another sexually fluid character, though never explicitly labelled. He is 'everybody's ex and nobody's ex.' While presented in an often-comedic way, he represents a lot of the preconceptions: that sexual fluidity and non-monogamy, or sexual promiscuity, are synonymous. Here, both Jake and David's take on sexual fluidity are valid and, most importantly, neither are 'conveniently' bisexual or pansexual for a storyline and then forgotten about. Their labels are both important and arbitrary. What matters is they're allowed to express themselves sexually and romantically, without judgment.

Clearly little has changed in the three years since Jake and David's first encounter, when he and Patrick accept his invitation for a 'whisky' (the alcohol metaphors persevere.) Meanwhile for David, he consistently mentions exes of various genders – or without reference to gender – across the series. One particularly lovely touch in reminding the audience of his pansexuality is during their tour of a wedding venue in series six, when he mentions an ex-girlfriend. It's a small thing, but it stands out; in marrying Patrick, he isn't erasing his pansexual identity, there isn't a refusal to acknowledge his exes of different genders. David's past is treated with equal weight as Patrick's. Somewhat comedically, David says, 'We've all been with a handful of other girls' to Patrick when he tries to defend the fact he hasn't 'just' been with David. That they've both been with women in their past isn't used to erase their sexuality – Patrick views himself as gay, and David's sexuality remains unchanged even as he makes a commitment to another man.

This distinction is important. Patrick's sexuality is altered by his relationship with David – at least in the way he understands it, talks about it and labels it for himself. The show could have left it open-ended, that Patrick falls for David, while having dated women in the past. But they make a very clear distinction that same-sex relationships are what feel 'right' to him, and that he labels himself as gay in coming out – as does David when talking about him, which indicates it's a discussion they've had off-screen.

Meanwhile, David could fall into the classic category of pan/bisexual people being labelled in relation to the relationship they're currently in. David doesn't become 'gay' because he's in a long-term relationship with a man. His marriage to Patrick doesn't erase his attraction to all other genders. In terms of representation for bi/pan people, that is of monumental importance.

'They might treat me differently':
Patrick and coming out

Patrick's coming out story is perhaps the biggest moment of potential jeopardy for his entire relationship with David, indeed possibly the whole show. Schitt's Creek might be a safe place, but it's also a bubble, and there is no illusion that Patrick's coming out will be unquestionably welcomed in the outside world.

Imagine Patrick, a man who has publicly lived as a straight man for around three decades, now in an openly gay relationship, looking at today's wider gay representation in coming out narratives. Whether it was seeing Ellen as the first 'coming out' on mainstream TV, or Kurt from *Glee*, or Marco on *Degrassi*, or Clare from *Derry Girls*, most coming out narratives centre on teens and young people, in high school or college, around the time people have their first sexual and romantic experiences. There's little out there for people, like Patrick, who take longer to understand their sexuality. While these teen-centred coming out stories are vital for queer youth, they aren't the whole story. Those of Patrick's age group now live in a world with increasing queer representation but may have grown up in a time of silence, fear and discrimination. There are plenty of 'Patricks' in the world who needed to be seen.

David is Patrick's first boyfriend, and so their whole relationship is also framed by Patrick discovering his sexuality.

He meets David when he comes to Ray's for a business licence, and soon after offers to help him with the store. After launching the business together they go to dinner on David's birthday and kiss at the end of the night, Patrick confessing it was his first time with a guy. Coming out also involves coming out to yourself – the early days of their relationship show Patrick revealing he felt 'everything you're supposed to feel', and taking the relationship slowly at first, as part of Patrick's personal 'coming out' to himself. It is just as valid as coming out to his parents.

Patrick's personal journey to accepting who he is seems to come from saying goodbye to his past relationship. While Patrick might have declared his feelings for David in his breath-taking serenade at the open mic night, it's only after ex-fiancée Rachel comes to town, and the conversations they presumably have off-screen, that it feels like Patrick fully settles into the identity that makes him feel, as he says to David, 'right'. By the time he says 'I love you', he's fully accepted this part of him. Coming out, understanding your sexuality, is – as David puts it – 'deeply personal' on many levels that might not be immediately obvious.

With Patrick's coming out story, we again see that it's a lifelong endeavour. Having lived in Schitt's Creek for over two years, he's clearly comfortably out; we couldn't possibly define him as closeted. What's revealed in the episode 'Meet the Parents', however, is that Patrick hasn't told his parents about David and by association hasn't come out to them.

The honest and sensitive execution of Patrick's parents learning his true orientation is a big part of why the show has come to mean so much to many. Johnny accidentally reveals David and Patrick are together to Patrick's parents, Clint and Marcy; it begins as comedic, with Johnny saying the wrong thing, and Roland making it worse through classically ill-timed (albeit hilarious) jokes. From that, there's a stomach-dropping beat where it seems Patrick might actually be embarrassed by David himself, aligning with David's insecurities. Viewers breathe a sigh of relief when, after David asks, 'They know about me?', Patrick confesses his fears about coming out and is obviously in no way embarrassed by the man he loves. The scene is the perfect arc from comedic, to chaotic, to a stab to the heart.

Patrick reiterates that his parents are good people, implying that they won't be unpleasant, but he is still afraid. We know that each and every time a person comes out, everything could change. For someone coming out later in life that's a particularly poignant element – Patrick's parents have viewed him one way for 30 years or so, and while arguably it shouldn't always be, sexuality is part of how people view us.

'What you're going through, it's very personal and something you should only do on your own terms, okay?' assures David. That line feels like an unlocking of something, an acknowledgement. Coming out stories often push the person to do so because that's what apparently makes everything okay. David takes a step back and tells Patrick its okay not to be out. He puts aside his own feelings, his fear of having to hide his relationship and any insecurity that brings up. He instead makes it all about what Patrick needs. Similarly, many other shows would force the moment between Patrick and his parents to be a confrontation. Instead *Schitt's Creek* and Levy put all that agency on Patrick. He makes the decision.

Often in coming out narratives, parents are framed as antagonists and roadblocks. While, rightly so, the emphasis is on the queer person, looking from parent's point of view is also a refreshing element.

Patrick's parents clearly say that it isn't being gay that upsets them, it's that he didn't tell them. More specifically, they are worried they've failed as parents if their own son didn't feel like he could be honest with them. It's perhaps a small detail, but to queer viewers it can feel like a relief to learn that their parents care not about their sexuality, but that they have not been the parents they hoped they could be.

Is Patrick's coming out an idealised one? Of course. It happens quickly and easily, with no discernible fallout – neither from his parents or his boyfriend, all of whom, whichever way you spin it, he misled in different ways. It's also an 'easy' coming out compared to what many in his position would typically have had. Even without malice, many parents would have questions if their child, after years in a serious relationship with a woman, came out to them. But in the narrative world of the show, there's no reason those more difficult conversations didn't happen off-screen. Maybe Patrick sat down with his parents the next day and explained everything, maybe they asked the awkward questions he hadn't been previously ready for. Maybe David too told his boyfriend how being hidden from his parents for nearly two years felt. And given the solidity of their relationship by this point, it's likely they would have. It's not necessarily the responsibility, or in the interests of TV writers and developers, to show every detail like that. It's a highlights reel, a way into a fictional depiction, not a documentary. And while Patrick's journey might not be usual or realistic to some, maybe that's the point? Why do queer couples' highlights have to include the harder times and conversations to prove its validity?

This is a show that is exemplary. It exemplifies what could be. As TV viewers we are conditioned to assume it'll all go wrong, because that has always been the drama of coming out stories. In removing the conflict, the emotion isn't any less honest. It's equally moving for those who didn't, or can never, have that moment with their parents, as it is for those who wish to have it one day. For those who dare to have it, it's there: hope.

For those who can never have it because their coming out went badly, or their parents are no longer around, it's actually a devastating watch. Much like how Johnny Rose becomes a symbol of home for parental inclusivity and love, so do Clint and Marcy. As in life, at the end of the day, this isn't about the parents, the reaction, or their town: it's about Patrick. In spotlighting that, rather than anyone else's drama, *Schitt's Creek* finally does justice to the emotion of a coming out story. It hurts to watch because it rings true. It's also hopeful because it rings true.

Chapter 4:
When one of us shines, all of us shine – the town as a (queer) safe space

While it's clear that the 'town without prejudice' grounding allows queer characters and couples to flourish, it's worth considering how this shaping – a safe space for people to be their authentic selves – filters through beyond the LGBTQ+ lens. What we actually see through the town is that when you make a place inclusive and supportive, everyone is able to be their best selves. As Moira says, 'When one of use shines, all of us shine.'

A queer space is designed as a welcoming one, a 'come as you are' space in which people are welcomed, accepted but also supported to be whoever they aspire to be. In the opening episode of *Schitt's Creek*, the lawyer telling the

Roses they could live there says, 'This town just might be your saving grace.' He was of course right, in so many ways (and probably in none that he intended).

Leading by example is the unconventional Mayor and his wife. Roland and Jocelyn aren't your typical Mayoral family. Working class, we assume Roland's father and grandfather before him as previous Mayors were too, they don't fit the typical image of authoritative figures. Indeed, we see it in Johnny's surprise on first meeting Roland, taking in his image, complete with baseball cap and mullet – not the type of public figure Johnny is used to courting for favours as a suit-donning, expensive lunch-having CEO. While Roland's unrefined nature is played for laughs, they aren't at the Schitts' expense. Early on, they're used to highlight the Roses' snobbery, or their new fish-out-of-water status.

The Schitts become become a way for the Roses to understand the place they're now part of. Roland and Jocelyn represent the heart of the town. They're honest, hard-working people who are fulfilled by their lives. They're fully integrated – Jocelyn running the choir, hosting social events. They're also shown quickly to be smart, empathetic people, from Roland giving Johnny advice on supporting his pansexual son, to Jocelyn welcoming Alexis into the high school when she returns. Later, Roland and Jocelyn mention their money troubles; they're met with help, not pity, or shame, or a sense that

Roland shouldn't be Mayor without wealth. The Roses step in too, giving Roland a job, going into business together, even giving Jocelyn a trial at David's store (even if she declines), or smaller things like throwing a baby shower, shows that the town is a leveller – everyone is worthy of help if they need it, whether they're a newcomer or the Mayor.

The town is obviously not affluent, and the Roses' quest to return to financial wealth could have sat uncomfortably in that realm of comedy/drama that likes to put less well-off people in particular characterised pigeon holes. Instead, Johnny's declaration at the end of season two of 'It's Schitt's Creek, and it's where we live' is the exact second I fell in love with these characters, and this show, because that moment feels like equality and inclusion as defiance. The Roses are accepted by the Schitts, and the Roses in turn see the Schitts for what they are: better people than the ones they left behind. It's the start of a real, tangible feeling of hope.

Jumping forward a little bit to the show's last series, we learn that café employee Twyla had been hiding a monumental lottery win from the Roses for years, to avoid them feeling uncomfortable. She confides this in Alexis, explaining the money wasn't as important as just wanting to live where she feels happy – and that happens to be the far-from-affluent Schitt's Creek (even though maybe her revelation technically changes that). Twyla didn't want Alexis to feel bad, which ends up sitting at the heart of the show's message: wealth is in the non-material things.

The town advocates being who you are, and no one is allowed to question that. For example, Ronnie – a gay Black woman – who would surely face prejudice beyond the town's limits, simply for who she is. Her life in the town is proof that the acceptance of David and Patrick isn't a fluke particular to them, but the overall ethos of the place. She's an integral part of the town – the only one on town council who seems to know what she's doing, for one. She's a businesswoman, and a well-networked and respected one, she's also part of the town's all-female singing group the Jazzagals, and seems to be a friend – even if it's the prickly straight-talking friend – to everyone. She gets pulled into Bob's dating adventures, is there for Patrick and David's open mic night, attends Moira's big film premiere – where her outfit almost dangerously steals the show. Her constant presence, generally despairing at other people's incompetence, is a joy to witness, especially when you know she's usually right.

So everyone in the town shines because everyone is accepted unconditionally, but what about insecurities and personal development? Unconditional acceptance shouldn't be mistaken for permission to stay stagnant

– characters in *Schitt's Creek* have plenty of flaws to be ironed out, inner conflicts to confront, and Levy also presents this masterfully.

For example, Stevie has a monumental decision to make when she inherits total ownership of the motel the Roses call home. Does she stay and feel doomed to live a predictable, small life (as she interprets it), or does she cut ties and flee for mystery? For Stevie, it's easy for her to overlook her growth or dismiss it. We're taught by TV narratives time and time again that growth means huge change. But sometimes it means acceptance or understanding what you need. In a lesser story, Stevie's best option would be to jet off to somewhere more glamourous than Schitt's Creek and start a wonderful new life away from dirty towels and clogged sink holes. For her, the revelation that she could do that, that she is more than capable of taking charge of her life, was enough. It's a little bit *Wizard of Oz* (a suitably queerly iconic film) in finding out what you needed was inside, and in your back yard all along. It takes the support of the locals she loves to help her make her decision.

Stevie's dilemma is a neat parallel narrative device to the Roses' original issues with Schitt's Creek. For them, the town is set up as the place they need to escape from, and for Stevie too for a time – whether through her new romance with motel-reviewer Emir, or another job. Through Stevie we understand a further nuanced idea of a town without prejudice, as a town that lets anyone live the life they choose without judgment too.

In this alternative universe of lesser shows that I've imagined, Stevie's lack of romantic partner at the end, and even more so her lack of children, would have her likely labelled a failure (or at least an unimaginative cookie-cutter cat lady character). She's a reflection of where a lot of 30-somethings have found themselves – unsure exactly how they ended up where they are but equally unsure where they're trying to go; but she's also a refreshing antidote to the lazy equivalency of women in glamourous big-city jobs in trendy industries being the go-to career path (hi, *Sex and the City*), and she's a reminder that for most people that isn't reality, and that's okay – you can still be truly happy where you are, if you have the right people around you. Most importantly Stevie refuses to change for anyone else; it's not that she doesn't change or evolve, it's that she does it on her own terms, and for herself. Within the safety of the town, what she has, who she is, actually is enough.

For all the that the town allows the natives to be authentically themselves, it also has that effect on the Roses. It allows them both to change, and to be themselves simultaneously, maybe for the first time.

Unlike the rest of his family, Johnny already knows what he wants. He's always been driven by providing for his family, and there's an enduring sense of professional pride. His starting Rose Video with $2000, and references to many a hard-working year, suggests his business career was as much about fulfilment as financial reward, something he eventually finds again in the town. In their old life, he never had chance to go back to being solely a husband and father, as we see he wants in holiday special episode 'Merry Christmas, Johnny Rose'.

While the town offers a blank slate for David and Alexis, Johnny is more concerned with reconnecting with what he lost in becoming Rose Video. He spends a lot of time trying to get his family out of the town, thinking it's the necessary quick fix, but it's when he's forced to put down roots, to help with the motel, that he starts to think differently.

When Johnny starts working with Stevie at the motel, he resists the instinct to turn it into a huge business venture. It's only when he stops repeating past behaviours that he starts helping Stevie out as a genuine gesture of kindness. He begins to find what he truly needs and learns that he's at his best when he's helping others to thrive.

Even when, at the end of the show's last season, Johnny does in fact make the motel a successful business beyond his or Stevie's dreams, he is selfless in his moves, deciding to go to LA with Moira, instead of back to New York as planned, as LA is the best base for Moira and her revived career. Her dreams, her successes, and the whole family's prosperity are Johnny's real wins – it's fair to say the town of Schitt's Creek taught him that lesson.

Johnny's journey to genuine altruism is admirable, but it's arguably Alexis' growth that steals the show. When the Roses arrive, she's at once the most capable to handle sudden change in lifestyle and location – she has lived the most independent life of them all (which still might not be saying that much) – but she is also the most ill-equipped to cope. She has a sharp mind and a whole host of skills, gained from global (mis)adventures. In season six, when she masters the escape room, in true *Schitt's Creek* style we see that skillset come together in hilarious fashion – and she learns she already has all she needs to escape. She can, after all, expertly get out of a hostage situation, as she explains frighteningly candidly, but what all of her romantic liaisons, nail polish endorsements and brief music career were hiding was the fact she is both intelligent and capable once given the chance to be – once she was able to step away from the idea of what she *should* be.

At first, she struggles to find her place in Schitt's Creek, as she's never had to sit still and figure out who she is. Being removed from her previous community of (ex)boyfriends, shallow 'friends', and acquaintances from her ridiculous travels, forces her to truly face herself and begin to explore her interests. From Ted offering her a job at his veterinary practice, to her going back to high school to finally graduate a decade or so after most usually do, Alexis is experiencing true generosity for the first time. Alexis believed she had everything she ever wanted before Schitt's Creek – she realises she didn't truly have people helping her. Twyla helps with every little life decision (and horrific smoothie choices). Patrick even helps out too, assisting with her college work – all without judgement or mockery. It becomes something of a team effort. While before it was just David, sat at home worrying about her, now there's a whole group of people behind her.

Alexis' story is also one of how love can enable success, just not in the expected way. In a nice B-side to David and Patrick's story, Alexis and Ted, though not destined to last, are still a success of a love story, and just as powerful. The climax of their romance is not Rachel getting off the plane in *Friends* and seemingly giving up a huge career opportunity for Ross, it's Alexis telling Ted to get on the plane without her and follow his dreams, as she goes her own way to do the same. Maybe Ted and Alexis will turn out to be Harry and Sally and meet each other again when the time is right. But if they don't? That's okay. It's sad, yes, but hopeful too. Because Alexis' growth is also Ted's, and he gets to put himself first too.

Alexis putting her career on a par with any man's is some-thing she learns from her mother, but truly taking charge of her career is also something Moira learns from Scitt's Creek. She has always been career-driven, quietly (or not so quietly, this is Moira, after all) more driven than her husband. Done wrong by a film and TV industry obsessed with youth, her time in the town gives her the space to consider how to move on, but also take control.

While she spends most of the time complaining about her new home, she also becomes part of it, and you know that she's effectively pulling the pigtails of the place she secretly learns to love. She becomes part of the town council, the Jazzagals, and directs the amateur production of *Cabaret* (after ousting poor Jocelyn who didn't really have a chance against Moira's need to lead). It's fitting that when she finally gets a celebration, a premiere for a B-movie film she got the lead in, the whole town comes out to celebrate with her. Much like her daughter's experience, Schitt's Creek becomes a safe place to try out being different versions of herself after getting knocked down so many times by the outside world. There's a moment when she looks like she's really giving up (Smoke Signals, season six) and that actually she would truly be okay with it. The time in the town has made her realise she can be many things; rather than clinging onto what she thinks she's lost, it's the springboard for genuine self-worth. Which makes the win, when she gets it and is invited back to *Sunrise Bay*, the show that initially brought her fame in her youth, even sweeter.

Moira needed to be strong enough to walk away from that career, from everything that nearly destroyed her, in order to embrace it again on her own terms. Her story here dovetails with David's – they both needed the town to help them heal from the damage their previous lives did to them.

Nobody would have blamed Moira for giving up. Watching the show in 2020, as a theatre-person with the career I'd watch become decimated, I felt for Moira in her lowest moments. Show me a woman in the entertainment industry, in any industry, who hasn't been told it's her fault or been passed over for a man. But the thought of a place, in this case a town, that builds up the people damaged by the toxic industries, toxic people they've been around – that a place, a group of people could do that, is a powerful feeling. When she gets her premiere in the town, instead of cynical industry types, or people who would have gladly torn her down for a bit of clickbait, she's surrounded by friends and family, and a group of people genuinely in her corner.

The Roses are all rebuilt by the people of Schitt's Creek, and then sent back out into the world, healed and improved. David, now happily married and content with his modest lot, decides to stay in Schitt's Creek with Patrick to begin their new lives together. For David, it's where he needs to be in life, maybe just for a little longer or maybe it's just where he belongs.

While we focus on David and Patrick's romantic life, the town allows them to live the best version of their lives in other ways. David has spent his whole life chasing both careers and friendships that never quite fit. His aspirations as a 'gallerist' never quite took off, and it seems like he was always reaching for the impossible and was never happy. In setting up his own store, Rose Apothecary, David dismisses his previous judgemental self, who would've thought it settling, or giving up. It turns out to be both the perfect business venture, and the perfect life choice.

The town as a safe space, much like queer safe spaces, works as a concept because queer spaces mean different things to different people. For some, it's a place they need when growing up, to help them figure out who they are, and what they need – like Alexis. For others like David, it's about realising trying to 'fit in' with other places and people didn't work for a reason, and that finding your place in the world matters.

It's a really easy life lesson, then: if you make spaces where everyone, including queer people, can be their authentic selves, then this filters through and lets everyone be their best self. Though the conversation here is about *Schitt's Creek* and its power as a revolutionary queer piece of culture, what this highlights is the idea of spaces where people can be their authentic selves actually benefits everyone. The show itself is a marker of a culture of inclusivity fostered from the top down, meaning everyone involved in making it does their best work. When you take away the fear of prejudice and replace it with support: communities elevate one another to be their best selves, and this feeling also snowballs, one person feeling supported and able to be their best self will support other people to do the same. Moira, as ever, is right: 'When one of us shines, all of us shine.'

Chapter 5:
Fashion, queer iconography and music

When we talk *Schitt's Creek*, the fashion of Moira is never far off, nor the variety of David's jumpers, as a starting point. As such, it's interesting to examine how through costume and aesthetics the show 'performs' elements of queer culture, and how these choices add storytelling layers to the show's narrative. Levy has been vocal about using clothing, design and curation as expression across the show, and so we delve into the use of styling, fashion and queer iconography more broadly.

'The Queen hasn't smiled since the '70s': Moira and camp

Queer sensibility, along with camp can be embodied by

non-queer people: think Cher, or even one of David's favourites, Her Majesty the Queen. Moira is a version of all our favourite camp icons – she's Madonna reinventing herself, Liza still going strong, or Cher on her fifth farewell tour. They embody camp aesthetics: over-the-top dress sense, a flamboyancy or excess in their general demeanour, and often they've overcome adversity and judgment, and endured. Nobody embodies that like Moira Rose.

In the tradition of every iconic camp woman, she is strong, has a unique sense of style and is in personality and attitude over-the top. Jack Babuscio in *Camp and the Gay Sensibility* (1978) argued that camp has four necessary components: irony, aestheticism, theatricality, and humour. Camp is also that line between fantasy and reality, which is where Moira professionally lives her life. It stems from her clothing choices, naturally, but also her way of being.

There's a long history of camp exemplified in the Hollywood stars who collide with reality. Joan Crawford shifting from glamour of the 1960s, falling from glamour but still idolised. Judy Garland and Liza Minelli giving the performance of their lives, totally over the top but slightly damaged underneath. These women become camp icons because they keep fighting but with a veneer of glamour as armour.

Queer people, like David, both embody campness but also admire camp female icons. In a sweet dual-layering of its meaning to the queer community, he looks up to and emulates his mother's version of camp. He dresses in a version of her look – monochrome but with a twist. That it's his own mum, that in his world actually *she's* the ultimate camp icon to reflect in his queerness, is very sweet, and very *Schitt's Creek*. But also, when you've got Moira Rose, do you really need any other icon?

'The girls': Moira's wigs and the self-fulfilling drag prophecy

Drag erupted into the mainstream consciousness when RuPaul first took *Drag Race* to the screen in 2009. Moira embodies a lot of drag aesthetic, from her wigs, to her signature looks, even through the way she speaks – the essence of drag is exaggeration, about defying society's expectations of how to dress and act, and being fully yourself, and Moira lives that in everything she does.

Moira's wigs are of course a huge visual part of her identity – 'my girls' as she calls them. They each have their own personality, which she selects for a specific purpose or mood. She doesn't wear them every day either – they are used for moments, or days when she needs an extra lift, or armour to undertake a task or face the world. There is an elaborate set of visual storytelling going on in every one of Moira's outfits, and along with it her hair and make-up, expertly crafted by Ana Sorys and Lucky Bromhead along with Debra Hanson's costume design, it creates the entire look. Moira's make up is still of the 'old world'. She was the glamourous wife and star attending events, and her old-school-glamour camp at work fits perfectly.

Wigs too have a deep history in queer culture and fashion. They are about presenting a version of yourself to the world, an exaggerated, more fabulous version. But also, about at once presenting a version of yourself you wish for, and keeping elements hidden. While Moira herself isn't queer, she is in keeping with the show's queer-inspired aesthetic and roots.

Moira's aesthetic would give any queen a run for their money, and many queens have adopted a Moira look: there was the infamous 'Night of a Thousand Moiras' drag night, which the cast attended. For one, in a self-fulfilling prophecy, Moira takes on drag influences and is adopted by queens herself from clubs to the mainstream – in RuPaul's Drag Race Down Under, Moira finally made her Snatch Game debut.

A historic backbone of drag is also the idea of a 'Drag Mother' who looked after and taught up-and coming-artists. They were schooled in their 'Mother's' particular performance style, but also given important lessons in life. On top of all the visual connectors, it's not dissimilar to the way Moira takes people under her wing in her own, particular way.

'I'm reorganising my knits':
Clothing and queer aesthetics

Clothing and queerness are closely entwined as a means of self-expression. For people who feel 'outside' the norm of society, who are already perhaps ostracised for being different, clothing can be a way to lean into that difference. Queer clothing is also celebratory of difference, a throwing out of societal expectations. There are huge and complex ways in which the queer community uses clothing – from categorising each other in terms of everything from music taste to sexual preference, through to a rebellion against heteronormative culture. It is nuanced in every gay 'scene' as well as across gender and ethnicity, but it also boils down to personal expression that throws the expectations of everyday clothing away.

David does that. While Moira's looks are more performative, mostly hiding a lot of her true emotions under her 'costume', David's are a more sensitive and nuanced insight into his personality. David's clothing evolves with him. On a really basic level, what start out as restricted outfits – buttoned up shirts, skinny jeans and leather jackets, morph into a softer selection of sweaters, pants and skirts, as David becomes more comfortable with his home in Schitt's Creek.

His sweaters and other clothing also offer signifiers to specific moods and moments across the series too.

Two particular examples signal the evolution of his relationship with Patrick. In 'Open Mic' he wears a sweater covered in orange flames – the first time we've seen him in anything but monochrome or neutrals – signifying the 'heart on fire' moment Patrick's song gives him. Later, in 'Start Spreading the News' when showing Stevie the house he and Patrick will eventually live in, and finally deciding to stay, his sweater has hands holding flames. That final sweater is an amalgamation of the open mic outfit, and the sweater he wears previously in the episode – a plain open hand, which Dan himself described online as symbolising 'honesty, truth, and openness'. In a lovely bit of visual cohesion, David's outfits tell the story of his journey to accepting this relationship is forever, from his heart being ablaze, to opening himself up in love, to when it all becomes fully intertwined.

Another season call back is in David's final sweater of the season, his black with coloured hearts 'Love' sweater. On one level it's a lovely subtle Pride-themed sweater, on another its colour palette harks back to the sweater from episode 'The Olive Branch', in that bold colours worn by David Rose truly mean something. If the flames are David accepting and committing to the relationship, then the shapes and colours are him celebrating it.

There are so many more little clues to his state of mind and it's a brilliantly subtle layer of visual storytelling. While it's an obvious commentary, it would be remiss not to acknowledge David's gender-defying clothing. There's a lovely moment at the end of 'New Car' when David critiques Moira's outfit and she says, 'It's your outfit.' They are in fact wearing the same clothes. Funny, but also a subtle point on the genderless nature of clothing in David's world.

He isn't trying to 'be feminine' particularly, he's just using clothes for expression, some of which happen to be skirts. Sometimes he wears them over trousers (also feeling like a fashion flashback to the early 2000s for many of us), sometimes they're just a skirt. Either way, it's David being able to express himself across the gender spectrum adjacent to his personality. Nowhere more so than his wedding outfit – it makes sense that Patrick is happy with his 'little suit' (as David puts it), simple, classic, traditional; David goes for something else. In keeping with his usual monochrome style while fitting his general aesthetic, the tailored, considered statement skirt and jacket is masculine and feminine at once, because clothes and people can be both.

The queer aesthetic of his clothing is about embracing all of that – clothing doesn't have to be gendered, but you can use it to express your gender or your queerness if you want to. It's something Dan Levy has exemplified in his awards show repertoire of outfits, from his Emmy night grey version of David's wedding suit, to his yellow Valentino suit for the Golden Globes. This becomes important for queer viewers too, seeing a high-profile gay man embrace gender-defiant clothing, and embrace fashion and expression which has historically been limited for men, both on screen and beyond.

There's a long and fascinating history of coding and clothing within the queer community, sadly too much to delve into here, but simply: styles of dress for the queer community have been a means of communication, and storytelling – in presenting a particular version of yourself to the world, in rebelling against gender norms, and in indicating what 'tribe' within the community you might belong to, or be interested in. *Schitt's Creek* utilises that nuance, from the lavish looks of Moira, to the expression of a simple colour palette.

'Simply The Best': music

Queerness and music often go hand in hand, and *Schitt's Creek* is no stranger to a bit of musical storytelling. From the incidental music of episodes being anything but, to the theatrical explosion and significance of *Cabaret*, to redefining a disco classic as a queer love song for a new generation, there's plenty to delve into.

The most iconic music use on the show is the re-working of *The Best*. The song has iconic queer roots, being made famous by Tina Turner's version in 1989 though it was first recorded by Bonnie Tyler, who, while less known than Turner in North America, is equally a camp icon (there's few UK drag queens who haven't lip-synced to her songs at some point). Patrick and David's song, thanks in part to the beautiful acoustic arrangement of Noah Reid, who plays Patrick, moved from a full disco-camp-power-ballad to become a new, gentler queer love song beyond the show.

When Patrick sings to David at the open mic night, it is the perfect musical bridge to show their relationship developing without having to say it. Beyond the beautiful serenade, there is a lot more at play that resonates for queer stories. Firstly, it takes place in public, in full view of the whole town. It's in the Rose Apothecary, not in a gay bar or other queer space. It also takes place with David's mother by his side. It's all as significant as Patrick's song itself. That we get to see David fall in love with Patrick through a song is beautiful. That it takes place in full view of the town and with his mother by his side – that's huge.

The song also becomes a through-line in their relationship, bridging a gap to the big emotional moments. The second time around, through David's lip-sync dance format (as he can't sing anywhere near as beautifully as Patrick/Noah, he's the first to admit), it's a hugely vulnerable moment. It's moving too, because it shows unconventional ways to be open and vulnerable in love, that declarations can take all forms, as can romantic bravery. The song is not a mere background choice to sit within the plot, but a vessel for the characters to say what may be unspoken, and further tell the story in the subtext and nuance of what surrounds it; the use of song becomes a precise layer of expression, particularly between David and Patrick, a coded love language in the details.

This iconic gay love story may have just given the world a new queer love anthem. Already couples are using it for first dances, and proposals, and yes, like David and Patrick, walking down the aisle to it. Here we see Levy's use of taking what's come before, and re-writing, re-incorporating it and giving it back. As a final piece of the fitting '*Schitt's Creek*' puzzle, proceeds from Noah Reid's recorded and released version of the song go to The Trevor Project. It's a lovely full stop to this – a love song made queer, giving back to the queer community.

Schitt's Creek is so rich in detail, and so embedded in queer culture, film and television legacy and the language of fashion that every sweater, wig and pair of really nice shoes deserves its own deserves its own directory of sorts (fun fact: since writing this, Dan and Eugene Levy have announced a tie-in book doing just that, and more). It's an added joy of the show to constantly find more meaning in the context – that the characters, the small details, the legacies they connect to, stand for much more.

It would be easy to list every detail, every reference across culture, that seeps into *Schitt's Creek* to build on its storytelling, but though characters may not skate through life, when they walk through them in really nice shoes – you can probably infer something from which shoe they opt for.

Chapter 6:
Willkommen: *Cabaret*

The queer threads that *Schitt's Creek* play with, from culture to fashion, can all be seen in one theatrical musical explosion; but in true Levy fashion, it's not just referenced, but expectations are subverted, reinvented and offered to the audience in a new, sometimes unexpected manner.

The Schitt's Creek amateur production of *Cabaret* primarily impacts three central characters: Moira, Stevie and Patrick. For Moira, we see an evolution of Moira Rose, the celebrity and artist, adding Director to her résumé. For Stevie, we see her out of her comfort zone to perform, eventually adopting elements of her character Sally Bowles, which will influence her life choices going into the next season. And finally, Patrick, who in taking on the role of the gender-and-sexually fluid Emcee, steps into his queerness in bold new ways.

Cabaret has a long queer history. Based on the short novel *Goodbye to Berlin* (1939) by Christopher Isherwood, it was later a play, before becoming the well-known musical and film. Most famous for two incarnations – the 1972 Bob Fosse film, and 1993/1998 Sam Mendes theatre productions – it is a musical that is at the heart of the queer canon. The stage production starring Alan Cumming and Natasha Richardson quickly became the new blueprint for the show, and seems to be the strongest influence on Moira's own production.

Isherwood was one of America's first 'out' authors and put himself and his experience of the queer underground of pre-war Berlin in the original story. The tale follows Cliff (Isherwood) through adventures in the bohemian arts scene, and through Sally Bowles and her job at the Kit Kat Klub. Sally and Cliff begin an affair that is complicated by the arrival of billionaire Maximillian. Depending on the version of the story, one or both of them have an affair with him, and Sally becomes pregnant. She has an abortion, and Cliff leaves Berlin just as Nazi power is taking hold.

In the musical version, we are guided into this world by the enigmatic, Emcee. Against the backdrop of the club, pre-war Germany struggles between the uninhibited, welcoming world of the Kit Kat Klub, and an increasingly dangerous, prejudice-filled outside world.

Connecting the dots across queer literary and cultural history, and giving it a new spin, was the moment I knew I wanted to write about this show. As a notable personal aside, Alan Cumming – while playing the sexually fluid Emcee – was the first person I heard use the term 'pansexual' and give language to an identity I was just starting to understand. Fitting then that it was *Cabaret*, within *Schitt's Creek*, that gave me so much as an adult queer person – a call-back to the musical theatre kid just starting to understand queerness.

'Don't Tell Mama': Moira Rose as auteur director

Moira's story and the contextual compressions with the musical start in 'Whisper of Desire', where the musical is introduced by Patrick mentioning his audition. Moira launches into an anecdote about her history with the show; from David's reaction it is clearly a well-worn one, Moira as young ingénue actress finding herself as Sally. Charting the much-convoluted course of Moira's career is difficult at the best of times, however if we assume this production was just before she met Johnny and her soap opera career began (something we assume was in motion by the time David was born in 1983), then this was either her breakout role, or another in the line of strange but obscure performances that make up her career. It's probably safer to assume the latter, and the image per-

67

haps of a second-rate tour of *Cabaret* around small towns of North America in the early 1980s seems fitting for Moira's career trajectory.

Like Bob Fosse, *Cabaret* was Moira's hat in the ring one last time, and it was one that worked. This dark, slightly strange film, in theory, shouldn't have been a commercial hit, but it pulled Fosse from obscurity; for Moira, *Cabaret* represented what might have been a swansong of a different kind – her career relegated to small town amateur theatre, had another odd, dark film not equally altered her life in the form of *The Crows* movie.

It does lead to that kind of career revival, in part. In season six when we see her stand up to her old *Sunrise Bay* co-star and producer, we see her get validation and justice for what happened previously. For women in the entertainment industry, standing up to both oppressors and doubters is a big decision and a big risk. Although the accompanying success of *The Crows* is part of this, Moira's taking charge of her career and her confidence actually starts with *Cabaret*.

It's also a great re-reading of *Cabaret* to put Moira (and not forgetting Jocelyn who as assistant director also did a lot of the work) in charge of a musical that has been most famously directed by men, despite having a woman's story at its core. Bob Fosse's work was embedded within queerness – his work from *Sweet Charity* through *Cabaret* to *Chicago* would star queer icons from Shirley MacLaine,

Gwen Verdon, Chita Rivera to, of course, Liza Minelli, but Fosse as a director, and a man, remained a hypermasculine, misogynistic, womanising figure as outlined in Sam Wasson's 2013 biography of the choreographer. And so, while Moira might seem more a Liza than Fosse at first glance, perhaps it is in fact the reverse – Moira is more than the camp icon: with the ability to be the auteur, she takes over the role Fosse once inhabited.

Reframing a musical traditionally directed by men and giving a woman the lead flips how we look at it – as yet, no high-profile production has been directed by a woman. Imagine a *Cabaret* directed by a woman, where the gaze through which we view Sally is not just the male gaze of her composers, and previous directors, but one that sees her strength. Within the show, and for *Schitt's Creek* audiences then, in seeing *Cabaret* through Moira's gaze – under the subsequent moulding of Dan Levy's world – is a queer homecoming for the piece. In previous incarnations, the actresses who played Sally in male-directed productions were queer icons – Liza, Judi Dench, Molly Ringwald – and that is also reflected here in our director. Queerness and campness are at play; the result is a piece of theatre that delights and subverts in equal measure.

'Maybe this time':
Stevie's 'goodbye to Berlin'

Stevie stepping into Sally's shoes offers a transformative moment in her own life. At this point she is questioning her life choices; she's upset, not because her best friend is engaged, but because she feels her life is stood still, and that she feels that she isn't good enough. When Moira tells Stevie to use that frustration in the show, Stevie asks, 'Are you talking about me or Sally?', thinking she should learn from her role's optimism, or gumption or confidence. Moira counters with, 'Sally, of course – you I'm not worried about.' Going on to tell Stevie she is 'very, very cool' and actually offers her protagonist as much as she could learn from her.

This re-reading of Sally through Stevie – and Moira's eyes – could be seen as an improvement to the musical itself too. Sally traditionally has been tied up in her romances to a fault, and can be painted as naïve or subservient in productions. In this version, Moira instructs Stevie to 'take our Sally by the hand and go out there and show those people everything she can be, if she were only more like you.'

Stevie isn't defined by her romantic relationships, and neither, under Moira's direction, is Sally. As she steps out to sing 'Maybe This Time', her microphone is set, and she is watched by Patrick as the Emcee. A standard piece of staging, with the Emcee as the all-seeing observer to the proceedings – however, there's another underlying element of making a declaration within the show's narrative: as Patrick and David's lives are about to change, under Patrick/The Emcee's gaze, Sally/Stevie makes a similar pledge. In singing 'Maybe This Time' she makes a commitment not to change herself – as Moira has just reminded her, she is more than enough. Instead she makes a declaration to take ownership of all that she has, and is.

In freeing Sally from direction of straight male directors and having a queer writer/director imagine how a female director may approach the piece, we get a fresh look at her as a character. We see what directors like Fosse and Mendes have often missed: Sally has it in her to do better, to be stronger, to open her eyes to the world, to be the star she wants to be, to break free from the men who define her – she just isn't given agency to in the story. And in taking *Cabaret* from the auteur director of Bob Fosse approach, it is her Sally, Stevie's Sally, who teaches Moira too that she can be who she truly is. After *Cabaret*, it's not just Stevie who steps up to what she's capable of.

In giving the part to Stevie, the most unapologetically 'herself' person in the world of *Schitt's Creek*, she imbues Sally with a sense of individuality, an element of strength and self-assurance that comes from Stevie, and again rewrites elements of what we think we know. The reframing of Cabaret as a musical, and Sally's story within, shows Stevie that she was able to be her own person all along.

'Willkommen, Bienvenue':
Embodying queerness as the Emcee

Patrick in his role as the Emcee uses the show as a punctuation in his journey to accepting his queer identity. It is a beautiful use of the musical to parallel his journey in this season, and indeed across the show. Played out alongside rehearsals, Patrick's storyline includes coming out to his parents, and his proposal to David. By the final episode, we see him stepping into the Emcee's shoes – or, more accurately, his suspenders and eyeliner – and witnessing a new Patrick fully embracing his identity.

In another narrative, another town, the fifth season would have seen a character like David take on the Emcee to demonstrate himself as being accepted by the town. However, Schitt's Creek, as we've already established, has acceptance as the baseline, and so, despite the surface level similarities, he doesn't need the Emcee – he's already gone through his metamorphosis of personal acceptance. Instead, the Emcee becomes a much more powerful tool of acceptance: one for Patrick to accept himself.

He originally auditioned to play Cliff, yet Moira – as much perhaps in adoptive mother mode as director mode – gives him the role he needs rather than wants. But not before an audition which confronts him with how far he's already come, and perhaps helps nudge him the rest of the way. Moira's direction, 'The thing you must understand about Cliff, Patrick, is that he has been with many women, but he has never derived true pleasure from it', is a knowing wink to the audience and Patrick himself, who replies, 'Think I can wrap my head around that.'

Patrick's character arc fits the Emcee in his somewhat ambiguous life and background, who finds refuge in an unusual place. In *Cabaret*, he is clearly an outsider to Berlin. We never learn his past, where he's from or much about him, other than he's somehow washed up in Berlin seeking refuge – Berlin being a tolerant safe-haven, the Kit Kat Klub a safe-haven within that. The parallels are clear. While Patrick is more running from himself than any risk of persecution, it feels that Schitt's Creek has become his own Kit Kat Klub.

Much like Stevie as Sally, Patrick has more in common with Emcee that it may initially seem. The Emcee comes to life when given his make-up and stage, off stage he is likely someone else entirely; this is perhaps what Patrick needed as one of the final puzzle pieces in embracing his own queerness. His previous performance at Rose Apothecary's open mic night allowed him to embrace elements of that for the first time, openly and clearly embracing his queerness publicly in his serenade of David. Much like the Emcee stepping into his on-stage persona, Patrick is in both instances able to embrace elements of himself that do not come as easily in everyday life. In his serenade it is the sincerity of the emotions for his new boyfriend that they are both having trouble processing;

as the Emcee it is a mix of the other sexual and performative elements of his newly embraced sexuality that have
sat unexplored. Stepping out of being someone who
David describes 'a business major who wears straight
leg mid-range denim' into the Emcee's suspenders and
eyeliner feels like the kind of exploration which links to
a newfound confidence in his sexuality.

The choice of number for Patrick in 'Willkommen'
seems apt too. It is the Emcee's – and Patrick's – declaration of who he is, and the world he inhabits. While
Stevie's 'Maybe This Time' will shortly be a declaration
of action, 'Willkommen' could be considered Patrick's
declaration of arrival. It is his own welcome, embracing
and finally feeling part of his own queerness, and a
broader queer community – he arrives as the Emcee,
newly and happily engaged to a man, he is out to his
parents who have accepted him, and he now happily lives
in the safe space of Schitt's Creek with his chosen family.
This movement feels like a culmination of all that, of
everything this show has set in place in which its inhabitants can thrive. It feels like a declaration of Patrick fully,
for the first time, welcoming himself into that world.

'What Would You Do?':
Significance of *Cabaret* in *Schitt's Creek*

Both *Cabaret* and *Schitt's Creek* challenge their audiences'
expectations, though they do it in almost opposite ways:

Cabaret shows the audience the darkness when it pulls back the curtain and confronts an audience with the reality of Nazi Germany. The musical asks the audience, as the character Fraulein Schneider asks Cliff Bradshaw: if you saw catastrophe approaching, what would you do?

Schitt's Creek does the opposite: instead of the darkness, it shows the light. *Cabaret* showed what happened when people looked the other way from oppression and prejudice, *Schitt's Creek* shows what happens when people choose actively not to oppress or be prejudiced. What *Cabaret* does is untie a conversation about different types of prejudice – antisemitism, homophobia, racism – and challenge an audience.

In talking about these two stories and how they engage with the concept of prejudice, it would be remiss to ignore the conversation of antisemitism in both. Anyone who knows *Cabaret* will make the link, consider the implications for the alternative the show presents: in *Cabaret,* there's a sub-plot love story between Fraulein Schneider and her Jewish suiter Herr Schultz, who are of course doomed by the prejudices of the world. Against that, in *Schitt's Creek's*, Moira and Johnny's inter-faith marriage is both quietly going strong as ever, but also goes uncommented upon by the town without prejudice. In placing the Roses next to this musical, it's a powerful point for anyone who makes the links, knowing not everyone is able to live in a place like Schitt's Creek. Levy does not labour the point in his show – not making any direct reference. It's actually a very *Schitt's Creek* approach.

Cliff and his story arc acts as a variation on how David describes Patrick a few episodes later after his accidental outing to his parents. Cliff has had a troubled path through *Cabaret* history which ironically represents his character well. As *The LA Times* commented in its celebration of '50 Years of Cabaret' (2016), 'We can track America's attitude toward homosexuality, for example, through the progressive outing of the *Cabaret* male lead, from reluctant straight man back in 1966 to unambiguous — if closeted — gay man today.'

In thinking about the way in which *Cabaret* is now part of the story of *Schitt's Creek,* another extension of its queer cultural legacy, Cliff and his story have been afforded another retelling, and also, a liberation – one which Levy pushes for with his work, pushing back against the fear that led to keeping Cliff in the closest for so long for fear of box office failure. It is a well-worn argument and one, in the broader sense, that still goes on behind the scenes today. *Cabaret* and *Schitt's Creek* are pushing boundaries, even if they take different approaches, to further acceptance and permissiveness.

It is also a poignant reminder of how far we have come, and how much work there is to do, that there was nearly 70 years between Isherwood's novel and this series, and fifty years since the musical, that a variation of this lesson is still needed. The use of *Cabaret* itself automatically integrates the show into the narrative history of that musical and its part of queer history.

Isherwood was a pioneer of his time, in both the stories he told, and his own visibility as a gay man. That both these things are still needed, and relevant is of course a sad reflection of progress in some respects. But also to put *Schitt's Creek*'s version of *Cabaret* into that thread of queer storytelling, also shows how much times have changed. The reshaping of an inherently queer narrative, into a show that lets people be their most authentic, true selves, and using it as a vehicle to tell those stories, feels like the most perfect evolution it could have hoped for.

Chapter 7:
Johnny Rose and the chosen family

Johnny Rose is to a lot of viewers a father figure. Fundamentally, he is a good and honest man, and a caring father, but beyond the surface of his place in the show, many viewers have adopted him, and what he represents, into their own hearts. In his writing, and Eugene Levy's performance, lies something deeply powerful for those who, often for deeply personal reasons, turn to TV to find their own version of family.

Chosen family is a hugely important concept to queer people – so often a vital lifeline. Beyond Johnny and Moira as TV parents, the show indirectly talks about chosen family in the way the town becomes just that for the Rose family. None of them have ever had true friends before, and the way the town becomes so much more than that, is a parallel to how, for queer people, the 'chosen family' of their friends becomes as, sometimes more, important than their blood or originally adoptive or in-law relatives.

The show also has a very queer, inclusive, progressive attitude to what 'family' looks like. Whether that's Jake's sexually progressive outlook, Stevie's casual romantic relationships, Jocelyn and Roland having another baby later in life or, crucially, David and Patrick choosing not to have children. Not having children – and David 'not caring for children' (as Moira puts it) – is a subtle, but vital note in the fabric of the show, and a statement on allowing people to choose their own life path. It's a TV staple that marriage automatically equals kids, and not wanting kids is something to be questioned, almost feared. In fact, not wanting kids is perfectly acceptable; more so, it isn't painted as a big deal.

The exchange where Patrick simply says 'plans change' in regards to his previous trajectory towards a nuclear family, feels like a revelation on a par with David's 'wine, not the label speech' because it's so rare to watch a TV show where the character who does want kids is the one who changes their plan. Perhaps small to others, as someone whose lack of desire for children has often been the source of derision, mockery or pity, I, and numerous others, can be grateful to Patrick for making us feel less freaks for not wanting them, for acknowledging that babies aren't a condition of long-lasting love either.

Important too is that Patrick tells David he'd be a good father, because of his good heart, but doesn't push it. David can still have a family, still be a father figure, much like his own dad is to others, he just doesn't have to be a dad in a traditional sense to do that. And that is the essence of the chosen family.

Johnny loves his family deeply and openly, more openly than anyone else when we first meet them. Despite some notable shortcomings in parenting throughout their lives, it's certain that providing and caring for his family was always a priority. It perhaps was misdirected into work and consequent riches for a while, and is a lesson in personal growth, but it was always there. Once they get to the town, Johnny is willing to do anything and everything to both support the family and try and solve their problems. The fact that he doesn't always get it right only adds to his endearing appeal – we don't need him to win every time, but he never stops trying when it comes to family.

We feel for Johnny as a parent, and husband, who just wants to do right by his family. This comes back around in season six when David, believing things are better now, returns to assuming Johnny can pay for the catering at his wedding as promised. Johnny's pain at not being able to isn't about the fancy beef dish, it's about him feeling like he's failing as a father.

It extends beyond his blood family. We look to him predominantly as the father figure, but his story arc really is about anyone wanting to look after the ones he loves, in whatever form that takes. For the Roses, the love has always been there, they had largely just forgotten how to show that in the day to day. Though Johnny and Moira admittedly struggled at times with traditional parenthood of their own kids, they leave the town not only as more involved parents, but having unofficially adopted Stevie and Patrick too.

Moira may not be a traditional mum, but she still manages, in her own unique way, to take Stevie and Patrick under her wing. Though we don't see a lot of her with Patrick on screen, in the same way she tells David that Patrick 'sees him', there's a sense she understands Patrick too. Cemented when she encourages him at his *Cabaret* audition, but also later when Moira quietly reminds her son to take care to 'nurture' his husband-to-be. Likewise, she quietly encourages Stevie in admittedly non-traditional, maternal ways, such as encouraging her to take nude photos, but she's also the one to take action when Stevie is heartbroken over Emir. Johnny certainly is a father figure to Stevie, but Moira is the one who quietly lifted her up to be the woman she grows into.

Not entirely separate to Johnny as a father figure is the happy marriage of the Roses. They are a 'perfect' marriage of imperfect people, and a long-term one at that. There's no doubt that Moira is challenging to live with, and nobody pretends otherwise, least of all Johnny, who rolls his eyes and exclaims 'Moira!' or sometimes a bewildered 'sweetheart' at regular intervals. Johnny doesn't understand everything about Moira, even over several decades of marriage, but, he doesn't have to, because he loves her. Equally, Moira is not above telling Johnny exactly when she thinks he's being an idiot.

By the end of the series, we realise their parents' marriage is what Alexis and David have, in a way, been looking for. Alexis doesn't have it yet, because she needs to become the kind of person who could have that relationship first. And David takes a while to realise that once he has it, he doesn't need all the other things he thought he did. For audiences, having a mum and dad on TV to look up to, and perhaps be a surrogate for what's missing in their own life, is a powerful thing. Not only does it give a moment of safety, but comfort also – whether it's that your own parents divorced or simply never got along as well as the Roses. We do learn from our fictional role models, as well as real life ones, and we do take comfort in them as well.

For different reasons, many viewers feel connected to Johnny (and by extension Eugene), and his relationship to all his 'kids' in the show is part of this.

Patrick becomes a symbol of finding a chosen family as a queer person, with Johnny as a figurehead. We see in the final two seasons that Patrick has slowly become part of the Rose family. For Patrick, the Roses are the first real example of a family that accepts him for who he really is. He feels a closeness to Johnny, and regards him as an important figure in his life. It's not that his own dad won't accept him, but that Johnny is the first father to do so. For queer viewers, whether their own parents have yet to accept them, or have rejected them, that too is what Johnny represents; what a parent to a queer child can be, what love and acceptance can look like. And watching him accept and care for Patrick, who is not his own child, feels like being accepted also. It's the idea that Johnny, or the Johnnys of this world, could accept the queer kids who don't yet, or might never, have their own parent's acceptance.

He's telling viewers it is possible, and okay to find those father figures outside of your own family. That sometimes they might need them. That they might offer something missing in even the most accepting of 'real' families. Reinforcing the idea that 'family' in fact extends beyond who you are born related to – Johnny's relationship with Stevie also encapsulates that.

Johnny and Stevie's is a relationship that evolves in an authentic and heart-warming, but never heavy-handed manner. Their relationship really begins when Johnny joins the staff at the motel, but his guiding of Stevie in the business world soon becomes an independent friendship. As time goes on, Johnny is there for her not just in business support, but also at the moment she gets her heart broken, and he looks after her just like he would his own kids – with slight awkwardness, but a pureness of intent. Similarly, when Johnny fears he's having a heart attack, it's Stevie who is at his side, and visibly upset at the prospect. It's a lovely element of the final episode that she walks down the aisle at David and Patrick's wedding on Johnny's arm, as if cementing her fully as part of the family. He goes from the slightly embarrassing dad to the person you'd want to be there in a time of crisis. For anyone like Stevie who is missing that father figure in their life, Johnny fills a void.

When the Roses say goodbye to the town at the end of the series, we don't see their wider final goodbyes – only the family ones. And that family includes Patrick and Stevie.

For queer viewers, Johnny Rose is a powerful figure. For many young queer people, their relationship with parents can be difficult. A father of Johnny's age, we might expect outdated views, or for him to think less progressively. Even in his moments of confusion or frustration for his queer son, he never thinks less of, or stops supporting him.

The idea of Johnny as a father figure is, of course, tied up with Eugene himself as well, who by extension became a father figure to many fans of the show. While nobody gets to really share Eugene Levy as a father beyond his own kids, the fact that someone like him exists in the world gives hope to a lot of people. Eugene shows that parents can be supportive, yes, but also the joy, happiness and kind of relationship possible with a queer child if you show wholehearted love and support.

What Eugene really tells viewers is: it isn't a fiction to imagine a loving, supportive father to a queer child. Johnny Roses of the world do exist.

Chapter 8:
You are my happy ending

The politics of a happy ending

Schitt's Creek was a vital, moment in TV history: the romantic-comedy-drama that ended with a gay wedding. It has been a long road for LGBTQ+ representation, and while it's far from over or won, it's one that owes a debt across TV and queer culture.

Still, in 2020, choosing to include queer narratives in a show, just by existing you become political. It's a sad indictment on the wider state of the world, but it's also true.

David and Patrick kiss 45 times over the course of the three seasons (and one bonus kiss the season before) that they're a couple. Dan Levy has spoken in numerous interviews about ensuring Patrick and David's physical affection isn't tempered, that they behave just as they would in real life – it's logical on arriving at work at Rose Apothecary they would kiss, it's logical that they would kiss at seemingly random times to show affection – because that's what couples do.

It's important too that the final episode felt like a true celebration. It's important too that the final episode felt like a true celebration, centring David and Patrick's wedding. Unlike many TV weddings, there is little drama around the event. There is *drama* in the sense it's David Rose's wedding, but there is never any danger it will really go wrong. The biggest obstacle to them getting married is rain (hello, Alanis Morrissette) but the audience never for a second doubts that they will make it down the aisle. Instead, the episode becomes a celebration of their love, the love of their family, and the love of the town.

The only other moment of jeopardy becomes one of both high comedy, and curiously touching in a way only *Schitt's Creek* can do. When David gets a wedding day massage that ends in a 'happy ending', it's both ridiculous, and utterly on brand. The sweet twist comes in that Patrick simply gets over it, there's no sense that this will derail their relationship or their wedding because their relationship is built on stronger foundations than that. Their wedding is one final, subtle lesson in both the person who makes you feel 'right' and it 'sometimes does work out' through a typically left-field example. It's subtly progressive, and wonderfully queer too, disrupting just enough heteronormative ideas of a wedding day with a 'happy ending' from a masseuse actually just going to be a really weird story one day rather than relationship-ending drama.

The wedding itself is a moment of pure joy. The whole town turns out to celebrate, singing them down the aisle to 'their song'. It's also a celebration of family, old and new, with Patrick's mum and dad by his side, his dad as his best man, embracing their son's happiness. Meanwhile, Stevie as David's maid of honour walks down the aisle on Johnny's arm, and then stands with her best friend. Alexis walks her brother down the aisle in a kind of thank you to all the times he was there for her before they moved there. And of course, there's Moira, conducting the ceremony in a way only she could.

David and Patrick's vows will hopefully end up on lists of 'most romantic TV moments' for many years to come. They're a typically quirky, but perfect celebration of their love. Patrick's are straightforward and to the point just like him – but also are a lovely call-back to other parts of their relationship. He says he'd climb mountains for David in a nod to their engagement on the top of a hill after a somewhat challenging ascent, and then sings Mariah Carey's 'You'll Always Be My Baby'. It is at once a nod to Mariah being the only person other than his parents David said 'I love you' to before Patrick, and in singing it, not saying it, references how he has always expressed his feelings better in song.

David's vows are more detailed, more vulnerable, and it feels like an important moment for him to say these things in front of his family, and the town. Until this point, everything from David has stayed fairly private, between the two of them. To go from the David who only said 'I love you' to his parents twice, to talking about his love for Patrick in front of the whole town is a big step. He tells Patrick, 'I've never felt as safe as I feel with you.' But that also applies to how he feels in life, in where he is.

David's vows also feel full of hope: 'It hasn't always been an easy road for me but knowing you will be there at the end makes everything okay.' It feels like a message to anyone still on that road, watching on – anyone still waiting for their Patrick. Significantly for queer viewers, it's the idea that our own happy ending is possible.

Promoting a happy ending

Outside the town of Schitt's Creek itself, the act of talking freely on mainstream platforms about a queer TV show, talking about a gay relationship, still feels radical. Networks know they'll get complaints; some, if you look at interviews closely, avoid engaging with queerness in their questions to the show's stars. Perhaps subtle, yet still there, and insidious; the fact many still avert their eyes to queerness shows there is still a way to go.

But then there's Eugene and Dan Levy; in virtually every interview together, Dan talks about his parents' acceptance of him as a gay man. The leading by example that *Schitt's Creek* have sought to do in the show extends to the creators, and in consciously including reference to his sexuality it is important representation. While it's no secret, and Levy is very much 'out', there is a kind of political activist side to people like Levy who choose to not only be out, but actively out. Some actors who come out rarely comment on that part of their lives unless pressured to do so; that is, of course, their prerogative, just like any other area of their lives. But there are some who, like Levy, take their being out in the public eye as an opportunity to raise visibility. And that visibility is vitally important.

A good comparison for Levy's politically 'being out' is Ian McKellen, a trailblazing actor who paved the way for the likes of Levy. What McKellen did, in being not only out but vocally, politically out, was force the hand of acceptance to some degree. While never going to change the minds of die-hard homophobes, by consistently being vocal and visible in his discussion of his sexuality, supporting causes connected to LGBTQ rights – an early patron of Stonewall, heavily involved in HIV/AIDS awareness and fundraising – McKellen forced the acceptance of his sexuality as part of him. Levy is carrying this on – it's a carrying the torch, again a queer community tradition – picking up from the previous generation, to make it easier again for the next.

That Levy also has his dad at his side, a man closer to McKellen's age, also being as vocal and supportive of his gay son, of gay rights, is a quiet indication of some of that progress too, in intergenerational support. Familial vocal support on a public stage. All of which feeds into the wider conversations the show has helped to produce, both in the media, and between individuals consuming that media, which is where the real change lies.

It's something extending beyond the father-son duo – the cast themselves are proud allies, participating in fundraisers together or utilising their birthdays for good causes, or attending Pride marches, whether straight or queer themselves. They're turning up, and making noise.

The power of the finale, of David and Patrick's wedding, and how it manifested culturally, is perfectly captured by *Entertainment Weekly*. On top of running several interviews and articles in one of the country's largest magazines, many of which focused on David and Patrick's story, the pinnacle was their digital cover series: Noah Reid and Dan Levy recreated scenes from classic romcoms as the cover shoot, *Sixteen Candles*, *Notting Hill* and *Casablanca*. What they did, on the cover of *Entertainment Weekly* for the world to see, was literally queer the romcom.

In downtown LA, on the same day these images were shot, Levy and Reid went to visit a billboard. Among the fairly standard set of pictures of the Roses in their glamourous attire outside the motel was an image of David and Patrick kissing; from the small town of Schitt's Creek, they now overlooked Los Angeles... 'Shine bright, friends,' tweeted Dan Levy that day. 'Very grateful for Pop TV and CBC and their support on this campaign that my teenage self would never have dreamed to be true.'

The heart of what made *Schitt's Creek* a hit is its story of love and acceptance. Whether that is accepting who you are, who your family is, where you end up in life, or all of the above. The themes of unconditional love, healing and family are all at the heart of the show. It also challenges conventional views of what love and family looks like but makes it very simple: the people who let you be your best self. It's a show about so much more than a queer love story, but for many of us, seeing David and Patrick get married, we felt like Patrick when he said, 'I can't believe this is happening'. But it happened, and there's hope for where queer storytelling, representation, and our respective happy endings, might go from here. In the words of David Rose: 'Sometimes it does work out.'

Afterword:
Best wishes, warmest regards

'There's a time and place for sentimentality…'
…and the end of a book is hardly the place.

The moment I knew I was going off at the deep end with nerdery for this show was Patrick's *Cabaret* audition. As a musical theatre nerd and a former academic of queer musical theatre, my brain near exploded. But also, as that sometime-academic, this show gave me my love of writing about queer culture back, just when I needed it most. I'd been told often that I wasn't good enough, and this book is proof that I, like David, am not a joke. It's proof that I won. Ultimately, I have, in the words of Alexis, loved that journey for me.

But so much more than that, over six seasons, *Schitt's Creek* slowly taught me about who I am.

On every level I felt David Rose in my heart. From being occasionally a bit *extra* to gender-fluid dressing to an especially anxious disposition. The episode 'Driving Test' is up there with 'the wine, not the label' in personal revelations, not least because I took my driving test six times (for added comedy, my dad was a driving instructor), but Alexis' 'nobody is thinking about you like you're thinking about you' felt like a slap in the face. I try to remember it often. I often fail. I've had more than my share of David's New York 'friends'. And hearing him describe so articulately what being pansexual meant, and living his life so freely that way, after years of feeling outside my own community, was important in ways I still can't articulate. At 30-something, to finally feel someone on TV understood you.

The moment I knew I'd fallen in love with the show was the end of series two, for the sheer joy in when Roland said, 'We can't tell our kids who to love'. I loved these characters, and I was never coming back. The moment I knew it would change my life was hearing Patrick say, 'You make me feel right', articulating something I'd never had the words for before. And later in his coming out story, giving me a way to understand parts of myself I hadn't. In a spectacular plot twist, I learned as much about my sexuality from Patrick as I did from

94

David. The labels on that wine might not matter, but it let me have that conversation with myself.

Patrick too, helped me come to terms with a sadness I didn't know I had about coming out. The power of seeing Patrick come out to his parents, because my own dad died before I could, and his track record before that indicated he would not be a Clint Brewer or Johnny Rose. But that episode is full of hope for me too, because it might help others get what I didn't.

That is why Johnny Rose meant so much to me. Because on one hand, I could feel sad that I didn't get a Johnny Rose in my life. But I can also feel hopeful, that the Johnny Roses of this world do exist. And for me, in the world of *Schitt's Creek,* I get to pretend for a bit, imagine I've got a Johnny in my life too.

To those people who want to mock it saying it's 'only TV', who tell me to 'grow up' and stop wasting time on things like this: I say that it might just be TV, but it matters to a lot of people, it matters to me. I also say that part of me hopes you never needed those stories that badly, to feel seen that much. But part of me hopes you do experience that one day, because finding something that speaks to you, whatever it is, always changes you, even in a small way.

For what the show means outside of itself too, many needed that. To see a gay man, as a writer and show-runner, owning his queer stories and fighting for them.

Yes, following in the footsteps of others who had gone before, but also, more importantly paving the way for others to come after. To see that man unapologetically be out, and proud talking about his show. The sheer hope in that, especially for anyone who didn't grow up with that, was so powerful.

Maybe it seems silly. But I know this story changed me; I think it saved me a little bit too. I know, without a doubt, this show got me through. Through all the damage that had gone before. This little show told me it was okay to be who I am. To be burned and bruised by life, to be the one who doesn't quite fit in, or who hasn't found their path or their person yet. And that sometimes, it does work out, even for us.

Acknowledgements

Everyone needs a Schitt's Creek, a place where everyone fits in, and 404 Ink are the publishing equivalent of that town. Thank you for welcoming me in.

Thank you to all the students who I have forced to go to 'Elmdale College' in recent years and listen to thoughts that ended up in this book.

Thank you 'Jazzagals' (and boys) to my Moira, relentless cheerleaders (even when I'm a diva) Kirsty Sedgeman, Sarah Whitfield, Steph Gifford, Fiona Noble, Rukaya Cesar, Beatrice Partain, Gonzo Millan Bueno, Sean Lyons, Mateo Oxley and Chantal Patton.

Thank you, the Stevie to my David, Ryan Souch, whose love of *Cabaret* rivals mine. The Bob to my Johnny – relentlessly optimistic in the face my cynical eyebrow raises, Martyn Wait, and the Twyla to my Alexis, always there with strange yet effective advice including to watch this funny little Canadian show, Janet Edwards.

Thank you, my Johnny and Moira all in one, my mum, Beverley Slee (and for putting up with me being 'a bit David' sometimes).

Finally, to everyone who helped create *Schitt's Creek* and giving us all a place to fit in, and especially to Eugene Levy and Daniel Levy for imagining a place where that could be true, thank you.

About the Author

Emily Garside is a writer of many kinds as well as a professional nerd. Emily spent a number of years as an academic and lecturer, beginning with her PhD on theatrical responses to the AIDS crisis, and the evolution of LGBTQ theatre. Currently she is working on two books related to her research. She now specialises in Queer Culture Writing. As a journalist she is a regular contributor for *The Queer Review* and has written for *American Theatre*, *Slate*, BBC and *The Stage*.

Twitter: @EmiGarside / emilygarside.com